The Cat's Tale

& CELL 13

SANDRA WOODCOCK • IRIS HOWDEN

Published in association with The Basic Skills Agency

Hodder & Stoughton

Order queries: Please contact Bookpoint Ltd, 39 Milton Park, Abingdon, Oxon OX14 4TD. Telephone: (44) 01235 400414. Fax: (44) 01235 400454. Lines are open from 9 am - 6 pm Monday to Saturday, with a 24-hour message answering service. Email address: orders@bookpoint.co.uk

The publishers and The Basic Skills Agency wish to acknowledge the contribution of the NEWNAT Project, Nottinghamshire LEA, and of the Project Leader, Peter Beynon, in the conception, writing and publication of the series.

A CIP record is available from the British Library

ISBN 0 340 52103 1

First published 1989
New edition 1996
Impression number   17   16   15   14   13   12   11   10   9   8
Year   2004   2003   2002   2001   2000   1999   1998

Typeset by Gecko Limited, Bicester, Oxon.
Printed in Great Britain for Hodder & Stoughton Educational, a division of Hodder Headline Plc, 338, Euston Road, London NW1 3BH by Redwood Books, Trowbridge, Wiltshire BA14 8RN.

The Cat's Tale

You shouldn't have killed me, Danny.

Oh, I know you never liked cats.
I know you hated me.
You hated me because Sue was so fond of me.
I used to watch you across the room
as I sat on her lap.

She loved me.
'I don't know what I'd do without you, Jet,'
she'd say as her long fingers skimmed over my fur.
'You're such a comfort.
We understand each other so well.'
I was almost part of her.

We were all right, the two of us,
until you married Sue. You cat-hater!

There never was room for a cat-hater in our life,
but I put up with you.
I kept my distance.
I had to live with your kicks and curses.

And then you quarrelled.
What a night! What a fight!
Cups and plates smashed on the walls.
Shouting, screaming, sobbing.
Then she ran out,
slamming the door behind her.

And you, cat-hater, were full of spite,
with your anger waiting to boil over.

How to hurt her? How to really get her?

The cat! Destroy it! Kill it!
That will show her.

Can you remember, Danny,
how you pushed me into that dark bag,
gave me a brick for company,
and took me for a midnight swim in the canal?
You made sure I was well and truly dead,
didn't you?

But you forgot something –
something everyone knows about cats.
Even a child will tell you –
a cat has nine lives.

So here I am looking at you across the room
just as I did before.
But you can't see me – not yet –
you can only see Sue.

She sits and files her nails.
Do you notice how she's grown them longer?
Her hair is different too.
It's almost black.
Perhaps it's a hair dye.

It looks good –
black and glossy like my fur was.
Her eyes look good too.
Is it just make-up?
She yawns, stretches,
rubs the back of her hand around her face.
She slinks across the room towards you.

You see me now, Danny, don't you?

***

Sue never really understood
why her husband had a breakdown.
She tried to make sense of his ranting and raving.
She tried to live with him, to help him.

'These tablets will help,' the doctor said.
'It's just stress.'

But Danny never got better –
he got worse.
Then he became dangerous.
After three attacks on her
he had a complete breakdown.
He was taken into hospital.

After she said goodbye to him,
Sue came back to the empty flat.
She sat down slowly.
She felt so alone – in need of someone.
Then through the open door
an old friend strolled in.
'Jet! Where have you been?
It's been five weeks –
I thought you'd been run over.
Welcome home!'

Cell 13

March 1st

Still here on remand.
No word about my case.
Jackson left this morning.
He gave me this note-book.
Will keep a diary.
Helps to pass the time.
At least I've got the cell to myself.
Won't miss Jackson's smelly feet!

March 2nd

Didn't sleep too well on my own.
Must have got used to Jackson's snoring!
Had a bad dream.
Thought someone was trying to wake me.
Letter from Mum.
Dad's chest is no better.
They won't be able to visit yet.
Shame.
Might ask them to bring my radio when they come.

March 3rd

The pipes in this place make a racket.
Kept me awake all night.
Knock, knock, knock.
Asked Roberts and Ball in the next cell
if they'd been tapping.
Ball said hearing things
was the first sign of madness.
Stupid sod!
Got a bag of matches from the canteen
to make a model.
Think I might make a gypsy caravan.

March 4th

Wish I could sleep better.
I feel so tired all the time.
Last night I swear I heard someone breathing
in the other bed. Spooky.
Got a letter from Julie.
God, I miss her.

March 5th

Started the model.
Heard that breathing again.
Gives me the creeps.
Then I thought someone touched my arm.
I must be going round the bend.

March 6th

Canteen day! Bought burn, sweets
and another letter to send out.
Wrote to Julie.
I put in a poem a lad let me copy out.
I hate the night time.
Try to stay awake as long as I can now.

March 7th

Letter from Mum.
Dad no better.
I feel useless in here.
Wish I was at home.
She hasn't heard from the solicitor.
Hope my court case comes up soon.
I can't stand this waiting.
Spoke to Smithy –
an old guy who's worked in the stores for years.
He says my cell's got a ghost.

March 8th

Old Smithy could be right.
Last night I heard this voice.
It said my name as clear as anything.
I woke up shouting.
Then the screw came and told me to shut up.
He said I'd lose T.V. time
if I made any more racket.

March 9th

Heard the voice again.
Felt the hand on my arm.
Heard the breathing.
I can't take any more.
I asked to see the doctor,
told him I can't sleep.
He wouldn't give me anything.
Said it was just nerves.
Mean old git.

March 10th

The gypsy caravan smashed to the floor
this morning.
It couldn't have fallen on its own.
Asked the screw for a change of cell.
He told me they were all full.

March 11th

Saw the ghost last night.
Still can't believe it.
This lad came out of the place where the sink is.
He was about my age. Fair hair. Dead pale.
He stood and looked right at me.
I felt icy cold.
Then he vanished.
Really scary.
Got another letter from Mum. Dad's worse.
I hope this ghost isn't a bad sign.

March 12th

I've got to see the Governor – I must change cells.
Can't take any more.
Last night *he* came again. Same as before.
Right out of the wall.
He looked at me.
Then he stood on the bed –
took his shirt off –
tied it to the window bars.
Hanged himself!

I screamed and yelled.
The screw came in.
There was nothing there.
God, I'm scared.

March 13th

The Governor will see me tomorrow.
Thank God!
Asked old Smithy about the ghost.
He gave me a funny look
when I said I'd seen it.
He wouldn't say another word.
What's going to happen tonight?

This diary was found in the cell of the young prisoner,
Jason Hill, who hanged himself in his cell
whilst on remand . . .
on the night of Friday 13th March 1987.